Overgrown Garden

A collection of nature poetry
By
Laurel L Mccue

Copyright 2014 Laurel l Mccue

All rights reserved. No part of this publication

May be reproduced, stored in a retrieval

System, or transmitted, in any form or by any

Means without the prior written permission of

The author

This book is dedicated to all of my friends.
Who inspired and supported my efforts.
Special thanks go out to
Tina...Nancy...Allen...Judith...Karen
Marion...Marcella   April and Sherry
And to Kevin, the love of my life

Table of Contents

Overgrown Garden

Garden war

Night and day

Sunshine shower

Sa-shay

Merciless Nature

Ancient Oak

Orchid

Fog Dance

Cloud Clans

The day begins

End of the rainbow

Sparrows

Circle of Life

Ode to spring

Scandalous!

Summer night

Fog

A Herald

Wind

Message

Springs Elixir

Stardust Stew

The stars are so brilliant

Garden Fountain Haiku

Recharge

After the heat of summer comes the cold

Patterns of Chaos

Cloud Dance

Young and feckless

Summer at its best

Incognito Haiku

Whetted Vengeance

Chaos

Sun

Quick

Who?

Clouds

Seeds

Adrift

Summer Rain

Butterflies

Crow

If Only

Cooing Haiku

Sunflower haiku

Dancing Wind Haiku

Blanket Haiku

Obliterating haiku

My Cathedral

Freshly Minted

A special Spot

Trees are built

Waiting to get burned

Natural Matinee

Where does spring go?

Fog drifts down

Gentle Giant

Heaven and Earth

Shout it!!

Mother Nature

Make Merry!

Day at the beach

Songs of Regret Haiku

Leaves

Moon haiku

Trees

Filled with love

Some flowers shaded blue?

Echo of Hard Rain haiku

Weed Whacking

Like a Drum haiku

Mosquito?

Country Drive

Summertime is Fun Time

Garden of Despair

The flavor of shame

Overgrown Garden

Overgrown garden full of charm,
I love your tangled shoots.
Designed by the Mother with care,
touched by spring, and taking root.

The flowers are thickly collected in blooms,
like tattered rainbows sitting on stumpy stools.
Dew sparkles, colorful tossed gem stones,
puddles of random riches forming pools.

Freshly tousled garden loam
signifies that I'm not alone.
There is magic running lose,
there's traces on every stone.

Over beneath the broken flower pot,
a tiny, green dragon lays her eggs.
Bees buzz, little helicopters collecting,
thick, yellow pollen on their legs.

Insects travel in caravans on unseen paths;
they have their own secret, guarded routes.
Mystic, mini cities, ruled by a queen,
millions adore her, hear their joyous shouts?

Doves and blue jays searching the ground,
eager to find the insects scattered there.
Fairies catch and tame these winged steeds,
riding high, on the invisible highways made of air.

A lone, tattered panther, feral and free,
hides silent, beneath the thick, abundant weeds.
Cautiously, waiting for his breakfast to arrive,
to survive, he must capture a living morsel and feed.

Over grown garden, so full of life,
I'm entranced by the activities there within.
If only I could minimize my ogre self,
I'd happily move there with no chagrin!

Garden war

Golden sunflowers,
bobbing in the breeze,
waving leafy fingers,
signaling for the bees,
Hibiscus neighbors also bob,
stabbing pointed stems.
Chasing away the fuzzy bees,
inviting the butterflies in!

Night and day

The sunshine is falling,
In glittering waves.
Drenching the garden,
With its golden rays...
Saturating the shadows,
With puddles of brilliance.
Washing away
In a flooding of light,
Night's gloomy grey cast,
A heavenly sight.
Proving once again
Sol's eternal resilience.
Against the cancerous
Encroaching of night
When cold hearted darkness
Will win the endless fight.

Sunshine shower

Sunshine,
Drenching my face.
Falling like rain,
Across my shoulders.
Dripping from my hair.
Running down my back.
Soaking my toes.
Sunshine,
Slowly clears away.
Leaving flashing rainbows,
Of white hot luminance.

Sa-shay

Beautiful,
Glorious,
late summer day.
I'm ready to dance amongst the flowers.
All the birds are singing.....
Sa-shay, sa-shay, sa-shay.
Come and join us.

Merciless Nature

Rain tumbling from the sky,

Pelting all the flowers.

Doesn't matter how or why,

Nature holds all the power.

Vinca's are embarrassed,

Bowing their lovely heads.

Lilacs meekly slumbered,

Tucked inside their beds.

Zinnias quietly bewildered,

Squat and hunker down.

Violets heavily bejeweled,

Turn and take a bow.

Jasmines are high-spirited,

Playing in the muddy bath.

Petunias hotly emblazoned,

Sway their stems in wrath.

Daisies sickly ravaged,

Lay on the murky ground.

Hibiscus thickly clustered,

Clinging tightly to their mound.

Rain flooding from above,

The ground's a muddy mess.

Flowers in a sodden mass are wove,

Proving to one and all, nature is merciless.

Ancient Oak

Ancient oak standing,

Stranded on top of a hill.

Contemplating life,

Been here forever.

Rooted deep in rich soil,

Living under wide blue skies.

Soaked by summer's rain.

Living alone by itself.

It's the only tree.

Planted by a young child,

Many years ago.

Lonely in its solitude,

Waiting for something,

Anything that will change things.

Patiently waiting,

The wind sings a lullaby,

Will the boy return?

He died a long time ago,

The oak doesn't know.

Time is meaningless to it

The tree is patient,

Waiting is all that this tree knows.

Orchid

Orchid on the wall,
growing from my cactus.
How can such beauty be,
among thy thorny vastness?
Your petals form a lovely shell,
a scent of heaven,
escapes to perfume the air.
I touch your perfection,
with my gnarled thumb,
and touch the heart of God.

Fog Dance

The fog drifts by lightly floating,
carried by the invisible breath of God.
It swirls and dances, an ethereal soul,
dipping and swirling, to a universal song.
Angels join the chorus.
Fanning their enormous wings,
pearly white, gilded with gold.
Sol peeks timidly from behind the embanked clouds.
Entranced by the graceful touch and go.
Weeping golden sunshine as he watches,
the eerie and tantalizing sight.
The moon rolls away all grumpy.
He's seen the same show,
so many, many times before.
Hiding his wan face, he pulls the covers up,
closes his cratered eyes and begins to snore.

Cloud Clans

I watch the clouds as they float by
high, high, up in the sky.

They come in every shape and size
all members of the same tribe.

Be they black, white or even grey
Together they dance and play.

They do not war, they do not hate
Religion is not upon their plate.

Together they float across the skies
painting pretty pictures, as the dance on by.

They do not murder, lie, cheat or steal
They have a wondrous appeal.

Why then, can we not get along?
Right all of societies, hurtful wrongs.

Be like the clouds and float through life
letting go of all that isn't right.

Join together in a happy dance
Holding hands and take a chance.

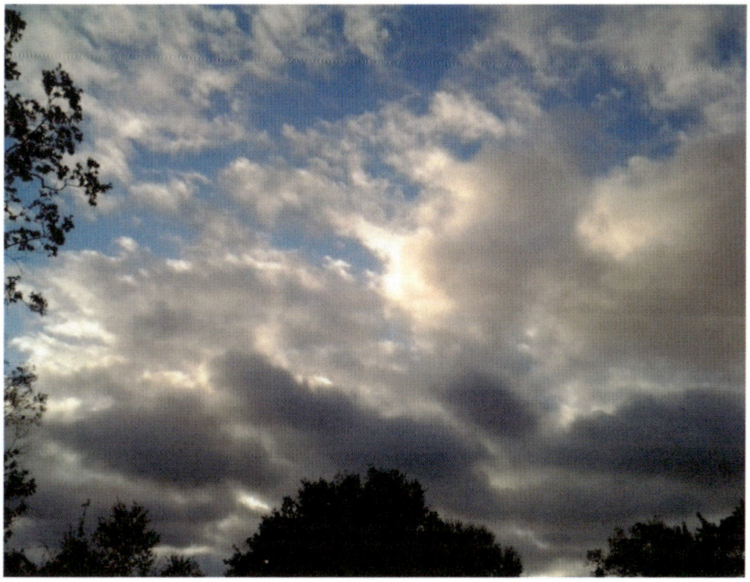

The day begins

The sun slips golden fingers,
Of softly glowing light,
Through the shadows,
Of evening's darkness.
He peeps above the horizons,
Red tinged line,
Waking the deeply sleeping masses.
Clouds floating majestically,
Towards the king,
Bearing royal treasures grand.
The birds break out in a joyous song.
Morning has come,
Once again to this land.
The day begins.

End of the rainbow

It rained all night,
and most of the morning too.....
The garden was soaked,
the puddles grew and grew.
I was feeling far too somber,
my heart it felt quite grim.
I went for a walk in my garden,
honestly, it was only just a whim.
I was rewarded for my efforts,
the brave sun made it out.....
From behind the dark grey clouds....
rays of sunshine hit my house.
And once my eyes adjusted,
and I could see again.
There appeared a double rainbow,
with my house at the very end!
So many brilliant colors,
of every shade and hue,
turned my house into a palace,
every feature was renewed.
Wishfully, I stood there,
drinking in the grandiose site,
memorizing every single color,
to store forever in my mind.
And my somber mood was lifted,
my grimness disappeared,
for such a sight is blessed,
and will last me all my years.
I stood there in the garden,
rooted to that hallowed spot,
and slowly watched the colors fade,
and my palace soon was lost.
My own dull home it stood there,
old and drab and grey.
But somehow looking better,
for having touched a rainbows end.

Sparrows

A sky dressed up in dullest grey,
misty tear drops of falling rain,
reflecting the world's great and constant sorrow.

Should I sit here and try hard to pray,
can I alleviate any of the pain,
and will there ever be a brighter, better off tomorrow?

I listen to the local newsman say,
in words both loud and grossly plain,
that life is one big bloody, bar room brawl.

I feel the heavy weight, and it's here to stay,
there are never any pleasures gained,
why can't we live like the simple sparrows?

We'd laugh together and join in play,
days filled with fun, there'd be no restraints,
Honesty, integrity, our paths kept on the straight and narrow.

Hearts full of gladness, and feeling gay....
no cause to grieve nor to give complaint,
wildly free, happy and trusting little sparrows.

Circle of Life

Snake flicking forked tongue

Slithering through the tall grass

Captured by the hawk

The hawk feeds its chicks

The chicks rejoice being fed

The snake meat is good

The chicks grow greedy

One chick over balances

It falls from the nest

To the ground below

It is soon found by a snake

A big hungry snake

The snake eats the chick

The snake is heavy with eggs

It lays them nearby

Underneath the tree

The circle of life moves on

Both species prosper

Interconnected

Nature's finest work

Ode to spring

The sun is shining quite brightly,
in a sky that's a brilliant shade of blue.
Birds gather in the brush to sing merrily,
an impromptu orchestra for me and for you.

Flowers smile and nod their pretty faces,
a living buffet of kaleidoscope gems.
Fresh new grass, our steps leaving no traces,
so soft there are no bent nor broken stems.

A light spring fragrance tasted through my nose,
the flavors of youth and carefree indulgences.
I weep with joy as my happiness grows and grows...
My heart and soul filled to bursting with springs excesses.

Scandalous!

Roses in my garden
sparkling wet with dew.

Lying next to lilacs
a perfect shade of blue.

Towering high the iris
shakes its head and mutters low.

What will the others think
seeing how closely those two grow?

A little dandelion
roars with laughter at the pun.

Knowing they'll never truly be together
not with those thorns so sharp and long!

Summer night

A smoky haze coating the edges of earth,
Dense swirling fog obscuring the birth,
of strange looking objects, emerging in glare,
Coyishly lifting her voluminous stare,
A reflection of moonlight, stars in her eyes,
This wondrous beauty a warm summer night.

Fog

Foggy day. Foggy night.
The worlds been wrapped in gossamer
enraptured and captured,
I stare in startled awe.
Trees are wrapped in misty threads,
Dancing to the tunes trapped in their heads
White starry eyes pierce the veil,
Revealing the neighbors daily trek,
to a far off land where work is king,
I hear their motors cough and creak
In the distant cover a tomcat snarls,
In answer another screams.
Their clash is revealed in bits and threads,
Through fog drifting softer than a dream.
White ghostly fingers caress my face,
Cool fingers touch my soul
shivers of delight race down my spine,
And play tug-of-war with my toes.
I creep reluctant back to my smoky lair,
Fog dust sparkling on my hands,
and recover lost senses,
Left in the fairyland of fog.

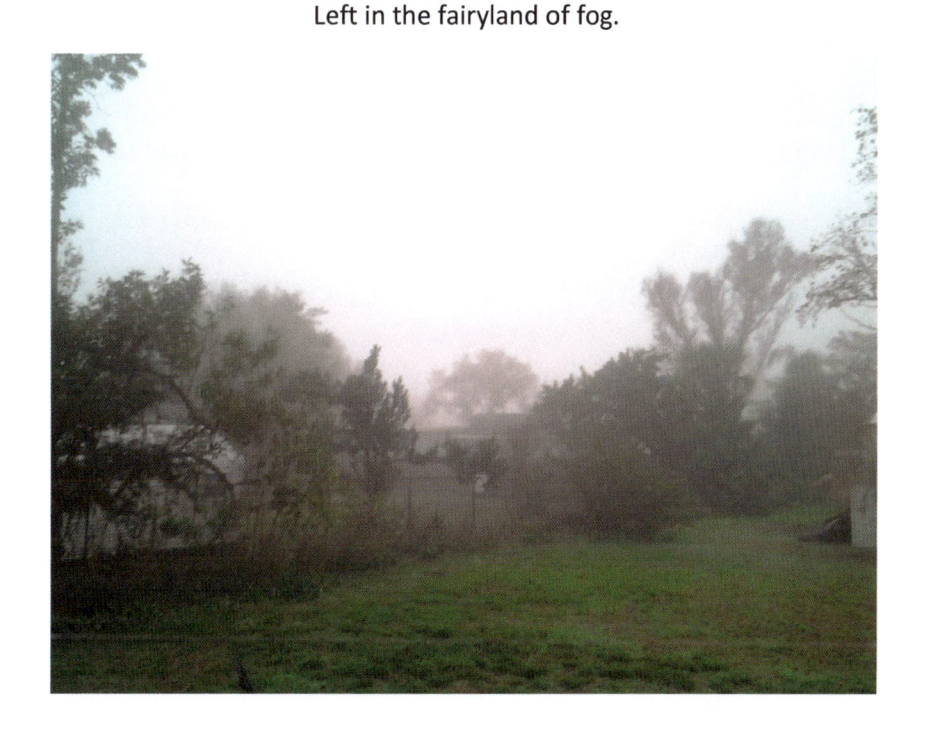

A Herald

A crisply cold, pre-dawn morning
frosted thickly in a blanket of glittering dew.

Sparkling bright little diamonds
scattered widely across the frozen ground.

Overhead the wispy clouds are soaring
in a pale anemic sky, colored a soft baby blue.

Mother Nature's way perhaps to maybe remind us
winter has us gripped quite tightly, he's hanging around.

I see a flock of brightly chested robins scoring
a peck of half frozen worms and bugs to chew.

A herald of spring's sweet oncoming climax
Flowers will replace the diamonds once harsh winter is unbound.

Wind

Wind screaming in derision
wanting to wipe clean the Earth.
Wantonly careless chaos
wild broom of the universe.

Wind moaning soft in sorrow
whispering through the trees.
Waking me up for breakfast
wispy kisses puff against my hair.

Wind whistling a hello
wanting me to come and play.
Warbling out a sun soaked tune
wrote a poem upon my heart.

Message

The sky is a blank page
colored cerulean blue.
God's messages are left on it
written in the ink called clouds.
White and puffy, swirled with a twist.
Jumbled with grey and black.
He scrawls across the heavens...
with his galactic pen.
Lightning bolts serve as punctuation
Rain lashes away mistakes...
Wind carries his message
around the world
one country at a time.
I stand out in the yard.
Sunshine pounding on my face.
Wishing that I understood
What God is trying to say.

Springs Elixir

Drinking deep of spring's elixir
freshly brewed in the crisp, clean air.
A rich bouquet sweet with blossoms
drifting by silent without care.

Throbbing song of hidden thrushes
better than any nightingales.
Fill my head with sweet surrender
as I traverse the garden trail.

Freshly mowed grass, green underfoot
velvety soft on my bare toes.
The smell is quite delicious
it covers the earth as it grows.

Bathing deep in the golden rays
delivered freely by the sun.
Feeling the kiss of warmth burning
my pale, white body as I run.

Breezes gently stir the mixture
blending natures given treasures.
I am drunk with untold power
Drinking deep of spring's elixir.

Stardust Stew

The night is a swirling sea of foggy mist.
Hurts my eyes as I strain to penetrate the cloudy goo.
So heavy and thick I can taste it.
An ozone flavor spicy stardust stew...
with perhaps just a splash of thunder.
Sounds are muffled by the pea soup
thickness of the dancing swirl.
It beads on my skin and feels so frosty
shivers ladder up and down my back,
as goose bumps mar the skin on my arms and legs....
it fogs up my glasses with a finely sprayed and pearly dew.
I dance slowly in the star light....
careful of the fallen cloud.
It seems to move along as I do....
partners we dance and sway.
The fog enters and becomes one with me....
I breathe in deeply...
completing the marriage....
Hitch hiking on a silver carpet of living breath....
straight from the angels far above.
The fog sucks away the soul with in.....
and carries us lightly away.....

The stars are so brilliant

Prismatic diamonds scattered...
Across a black velvet sky...
Throbbing and pulsing with light
they twinkle with mirth
strobbing their joy
at being alive
and free to play tag
on a cosmic scale.

I long to join their dance
clad only in the skin
that I was born in....
To bath in their glory...
to conquer the universe
in a screaming yodel of ecstasy...

I would capture and ride comets...
Tame them to my will...
I'd travel faster than light
astride
my astral steed.
And sow life amongst
the far off reaches of space...

All night would be spent
exploring the wonders of this universe...
As the stars slowly faded away...

Doomed by the rising orb of fire
the sun...
I would return to my home,
don my dull existence,
and drink a glass of tang...

Garden Fountain Haiku

water cascading

from a small garden fountain

lost in a down pour

Recharge

Sunshine melting my skin
to a brown and freckled hue.
A westerly breeze tickles
the clouds in a sky of blue.

A faint throb of traffic
pulses in my inner ear.
Fading and reengaging
it sounds so very near.

Hibiscus blooms opening
wide to drink the morning sun.
Sweat splashes down my back
a river on the run.

Deep, deep sigh of contentment
head bowed under heavens grace.
No strife nor conflict stirring
at peace with the human race.

Tick, tock, a ticking clock
my time is drawing to an end.
The advancement of age
a swift and terminal trend.

The westerly breeze is soothing
fingers caress my brittle hair.
Softly whispering voices
leave me floating without care.

Hibiscus blooms wisely bobbing
red petals clapping in surprise.
They see the truth reflecting
from my age worn, pale blue eyes.

Bolstered by my trip through nature
I shake off my burden of fear.
Picking a bouquet of bright hopes
I fill my basket with good cheer!

After the heat of summer comes the cold

After the heat of summer comes the cold.
Season's bridged by fall's cool Picasso sprawl.
No! Don't bother...I will not be consoled!

Blooms fading away, tragic to behold.
Shorter days and longer nights takes its toll.
After the heat of summer comes the cold.

Summers glory by autumn is extolled.
Kaleidoscopic leaves of color fall.
No! Don't bother...I will not be consoled!

Behind this show winter waits to unfold.
Soon ice and snow will hold us in their thrall.
After the heat of summer comes the cold.

Cannot the sunny season be paroled?
What deity must I award a call?
No! Don't bother...I will not be consoled!

Cruel winter's arctic freeze needs put on hold.
Its bitter icy season soon will maul.
After the heat of summer comes the cold.
No! Don't bother...I will not be consoled!

Patterns of Chaos

Patterns of chaos
dotting the sky.
Like sprinkles
tossed into, a heavenly eye.

Glitter and gloss
psychedelic toss
a salad mix of color
nature, representing my loss.

Twisted and warped
wind whipped into curls.
Shattered and tattered
slivered into, cute little twirls.

Mouth hanging wide open
a collector of flies...
Patterns of chaos
dotting the sky.

Cloud Dance

Clouds dancing on the breeze
racing from the rising sun.
Looking over puffy shoulders
to gather rain drops on the run.

Sunlight piercing through the veil
fingertips made of golden light.
Like a celestial lamp left burning
such an awe inspiring sight.

Invisible to the naked eye
the wind plays with cloudy toes.
Snatching and catching them
as the clouds dance to and fro.

Young and feckless

The dawn is ripe with promise
anticipation flavoring each breath.
There's golden opportunity
ripened by the moons cold death.

I smell a sudden crispness
heralding a little something new.
The clouds are all lined in silver
the sky is colored a brilliant blue.

Hope paints my world in rainbows
a kaleidoscope of possibilities
newly dawned ambition
free from all responsibilities.

I'm feeling young and feckless
as I face the morning sun.
Ready to face today's adventures
to live large and have some fun!

Summer at its best

Brilliant sunshine

Hot as hot can be…

I'm sitting here laughing,

Laughing at the heat.

I think it's really funny

As I watch the temperature rise.

I see a bunch of heat waves

Shimmering off the cobbled drive.

The sun is merciless.

It's beating against the earth.

Everything is sweating

Except for me of course.

Not one cloud up in the sky

To shield one from the heat.

The trees are limp and breathless

No breeze to cool their leaves.

The birds are all in hiding

The feeder hasn't a single guest.

It's like an oven out there

This is summer at its best!

My grin keeps on expanding

I'm joyful to the core.

Don't have to go out in it.

Yesterday I did my chores.

Weed whacking and some raking

I picked up all the trash.

I spread the grass and weed killer

Insects gave me quite a rash.

Yesterday I could not escape it

I had to work in the furnace blast.

So hard to draw in each breath

The airs hot enough to make me gasp.

My skin quickly reached a sizzle.

I sweated off at least five pounds.

The blazing sun got in my head

As I worked the heated ground.

Today I'm doing housework

I'm happy as can be.

Although it's burning up outside

I'm keeping my cool in the A/C!

Incognito Haiku

blossoms hiding low

beneath a carpet of grass

incognito plants

Whetted Vengeance

Clouds sulking across open sky
pregnant, angry and fulsome grey.
Lightning bolts loudly exclaiming
a storm is festering this way.

Wind moaning with dark desire
reconnoitering on the roof!
Sol hiding his one golden eye
imputing that he is aloof?

A scatter of icy hail falls
bouncing against the hallowed ground.
Jealous rain exploding sideways
makes a disjointed drumming sound.

Wind howling with a mindless rage
breaking ancient trees into two.
Roads deploying liquid sunshine
do not know what I need to do.

While heaven is opened up wide
delivering whetted vengeance.
I'm hiding in my mobile home
whispering words of repentance.

Chaos

Corrupted breath of an angel's sigh
whisking puffy clouds overhead.
Scouring through the heavens high
dropping low, kissing Earth
collecting flotsam
in unseen hands
scattering
chaos
Wind

Sun

Yellow orb of molten destiny
so bright it burns away your sight
center of our universe
overhead shining light
energy for plants
sunburn maker
looking
blazing
Sun

Quick

Quick
garden
from a bag.
Easy to do
they last forever.
Buy them at any store.
Many different colors.
Just stick them in the dirt, you're done.
Plastic flowers do not need care.
Instant garden, no hassles, always bright!

Who?

Who whimpers like a whimsical child
when whistling a walloping old timey waltz?
Why wincing as it weaves with a whoosh and a whorl
whipping the windswept and weathered wasteland?
Who's wrapping wrathful whirlwinds in a wild-goose chase
wailing woefully like a wizened old woman?
Wherein its world shaking, worrisome, walloping wind!

Clouds

Coasting lightly through the sky.
Catching every fragrant breeze.
Curdled a dark grey, heavy with rain drops,
Created by nature, crafted by her hand daily
Collecting in drifts miles above the dusty Earth.
Crusty with thunder, winking lightning bolts as they blink.

Seeds

Sunshine scalding my bare pink skin
as I work the soil in my garden.
Droplets of sweat splashing down like rain
watering the earth with my essence.
Fingernails packed solid with mother earth
as I claw at her surface with a vengeance.
All this effort for a few small seeds
designed to fill my winter with a splash of color.
An old blue jay hopping across my eves
calculates my every little move.
He's eager to feed on the tender feast
the sly old fox is merely waiting for me to move.
Weeds piled high, dirty scraped up knees
my clothes soaked with honest sweat.
Soon I'll go back to my air conditioned room
and give that blue buzzard a chance while I rest.

Adrift

Adrift
all alone
floating down
a quiet river.
Hand trailing in the water
watching the banks
on either side
as they slowly pass by.

Watching
a cluster of clouds
floating overhead.
Mostly white and puffy
like twisted marshmallows.
Some are darker
silver linings gleaming
in the vast reaches of sky.

Listening
as the water beneath me
burbles gently
telling me secrets.
Singing a lullaby
sweet and loving,
tinkling blue bells
played by unseen fairies.

Fish flash
sparkling like diamonds.
Scales catching the rays
reflecting the sun.
Filling the water
with bars of gold beneath the surface.
Rare riches
so far from either shore.

Sunshine
caressing my troubled spirit
touching my soul,
with life giving light.

Dissolving the darkness
as my boat rocks in the water
relaxing the tension
easing the strife.

Summer Rain

A tingle of static
electricity
filling the air.

The storm dances
horizon to horizon.
Bowing low.

Thunder rumbles
vibrating my bones
shaking my teeth.

Ozone flavors
the gusty breezes
lingering on my tongue.

Shocking brilliance
the sky stitched
with lightning bolts.

Howling gust
carrying big drops
of summer rain.

I stand in the parking lot
groceries forgotten
Enjoying the show.

Butterflies

light
fragile
butterfly
floating gently
across sun lit fields
riding a summer breeze
pausing to sip sweet nectar
from petaled cups richly adorned
in a kaleidoscope of colors
a buffet freely given and shared
sipping only what is needed
there's plenty to go around
butterflies do not think
about tomorrow
all that matters
is the here
and now
Joy.

Crow

A murder of crows cruising blue sky
riding stray breezes with spread wings
eyes bright with intelligence
master of their domain
bellies full of corn
black feathered thief
flapping wings
cawing
crow

If Only

Stretching up
high
on tip toes
playing tag
with the morning sun.

Feeling warmth
drench
my happy face
enraptured
by the captured rays.

If only
days
all started
filled with joy
dancing neath the sun.

Cooing Haiku

turtle dove cooing

lullabies softly whispered

for sleepy nestlings

Sunflower haiku

sunflower standing

alone in a rural field

leaves waving in breeze

Dancing Wind Haiku

cauliflower clouds

piled high up in the sky

dancing with the wind.

Blanket Haiku

pink flower blossoms

dropping petals on the ground

quilting a blanket

Obliterating haiku

rain slashing through clouds

obliterating the sun

racing towards the ground

My Cathedral

My cathedral
isn't very fancy.
It never has a crowd.
It's off inside
the deep, dark woods.
I go there all alone.
Sitting myself beneath
the intertwined branches
in a natural clearing.
I pray for guidance
and compassion.
Though the floor
is naught but dirt
a fallen log
the only pew.
There is something here.
Something bigger
and better than man.
Kneeling in this
hallowed place
surrounded on all sides
by natures gentle hand,
it's so easy to believe.
To become one
with my surroundings.
To listen and somehow
become a better person.
The swish of wind
through the ancient oaks
catching my attention.
The creaking boughs
and leafy limbs
sharing secrets.
I know that
no matter what
I'll soon come back again.

.

Freshly Minted

A new day freshly minted
pregnant with options...
heavy with hope...
sparking adventures...

All things are possible
energy abounds...
emotion runs high...
all will be ventured.

Dawn deliciously crisp
passions are raising...
my list getting long...
dreams richly tendered.

A special Spot

When times are bad
and morale is low
there's a special spot
that I like to go.
Shady overhead
splashing brook below
fragrant flowers
in a carpet grow.
A soft, genteel breeze
lifts my hair just so
I breathe deep of peace
catch the rainbow glow.
A terra cotta statue
with a child's brow
apples in both cheeks
waist bent in a bow.
Blesses me with happiness
cares and loves me so
His smile weeps radiant
joy upon the sparrows.

Trees are built

Trees are built of poetry
it's written into every bough.
Recorded into each twist and fork
all part of a greater whole.

From the color of it's trunk
to each leaf upon its limbs
every inch of a tree is covered
by natures poetic whims.

When the leaves are rustling
in a gentle morning breeze
listen closely you'll hear the poems
recited by the nearest tree.

Wandering through the forest
you'll be treated to some fun,
As a million poems are recited
blending into natures soothing song.

Waiting to get burned

The moon is so big this morning......
It's filling the darkness with light.
Moon beams so brilliant
they hurt my eyes.
Everything out there
surrounded with aura...
it's a living splash
of non-color
unearthly
glowing
pulsing with chaos
strange shadows
following my
every step.
I cower
within the spotlight
of moonshine
waiting
to get burned....

Natural Matinee

The drumming of rain
against a tin roof
complements
the gentle moan
of a tropical gust.
The moon glow reflected
from a thousand drops.
Sparkling gems
Descending from heaven
enriching my soul
with heartfelt joy.

Where does spring go

Where does spring go?
When winter grips the land?
Is she vacationing in New Mexico, perhaps the Rio Grande?

Is she busy with a lover,
or making some new friends?
What happens if she leaves us, and doesn't come again?

Or has winter bribed her,
paid her off in spades?
Is she hiding incognito, and wearing silly shades?

How does she cope with winter,
this lovely lady spring?
Does she make the icy cold one, want to dance and sing?

What are her secret motives,
when will her season start?
Can anyone so old and ancient, truly have a heart?

We're left waiting to discover,
just what the girl will do.
All of us quite anxious, to see old man winter shoo!

Fog drifts down

The fog
drifts down
coating the world
blurring the edges
making faces
as it floats
Slowly
by my window.

Catching the light
and leaving
pale traces
of itself.

Stately
and elegant
twirling
in the breeze.

Making known
its independent nature
as it goes.

Tingling cool
against my skin
making goose bumps
start to grow

Leaving a hint
of musty dampness.

I'm awkward
without full vision
everything looks strange
in this living glow.

A fantasy land
of lacy tendrils
draped across
the landscape
I've come to know.

I breathe it
deep inside
my lungs

Feeling the crisp
effervescence
tasting a hint

Of the collective cosmos
dancing within the banks
of the fallen clouds
that we call fog.

Gentle Giant

Ancient being
I am your humble servant.
I honor your age
your knowledge
your peaceful ways...
I thank you for your gifts.
Shading me from the sun
on a summer's day.
Filling my life with beauty.
Filling my belly with sustenance.
I hail thee gentle giant.
I am honored by your presence.
There are many others like you
but you alone are mine.
You shield my home with your body
lull me to sleep with your songs.
With any luck after I pass
from this, my world...
I will spend eternity
buried at your feet.
Comforted for all time
by your soothing ways.
My decaying remains
feeding and becoming one
with your essence.
Will I understand then?
Will I speak the language
of the deep forest?
Will I learn the meaning
of every tangled limb?
Will I become a part of you?
Will my patience be rewarded?
May I then become a tree?
I can only hope.

Heaven and Earth

The sky is grey and glooming
sprinkled tears are softly shed.
The angels weeping quietly
mourning the year so newly dead.
The fairies are quite cheerful
dancing and full of glee.
Celebrating the birthing
of a brand new year instead.

Shout it!!

Splashed with drops of vivid colors,
That carries all the tart flavors, of early spring.
I giggle, laugh and dance with the fresh, crisp blooms;
The red-breasted robins softly sing.... "For joy...for joy....
Winter is at an end, gone along with his heartless icy sting.
Smiling rainbows at the heralds, as they strut about,
Waiting gladly for the arrival of the wee fairy-king.
Shout it far and shout it wide, and listen,
With your soul wide opened,
It will quiver your heart-strings.
Welcome the new season, welcome life!

Mother Nature

Mother Nature Swirling, Twirling,

Lighter than a butterflies wing,

Prismatic colors bleeding,

As she lightly sways and sings

A scent of rapture tickling,

Blossoms as she whirls softly past,

A squeeze of fairy dust sprinkled,

Coating every leafy branch.

The awakening of life's forces,

Conducted by the Mothers hand,

Brings exotic scent and cobbled sweetness,

Across every inch of her great land!

Make Merry!

Make merry with the marigolds....

Dance and laugh and sing!

Soon frost will come to the garden....

And happiness takes wing!

Summer is a blessing....

Filled with joyful things....

Wintertime is stressful...

Gone the sweet and luscious greens.

Make merry with the marigolds....

Drop your clothes and drink the sun.

Don't worry about tomorrow,

It's time to have some fun!

Day at the beach

Waves slapping against the shore
soaking into the bone white beach
leaving trails of dirty grey froth
stranded like shipwrecks on the sand
as far as the eye can see.

Gulls jarring the silence with their screams
soaring on the brisk flowing breeze
looking for scraps and tidbits to eat
dive bombing innocent sun bathers
in their maniacal greed.

Plovers playing catch me if you can
chasing the waves as they leave the shore
looking for little fishes as they run
changing direction when the waves turn around
scared to get their feet wet.

Sunshine sharply glaring down
the sand holding the sky given heat
burning peoples feet as they walk
cooking their tender skins
a crisp and golden brown.

Children splashing ankle deep
laughing as only children can
building sand castles with miniature hands
looking for sea shells along the way
like puppies they only want to play.

No one is swimming out in the sea
jelly fish have washed in towards shore
in the distance a shark's fin breaks the waves
flesh eating bacteria wait in the wings
welcome to Florida's golden shores!

Songs of Regret Haiku

moaning of the wind

filling my heart full of tears

sad songs of regret

Leaves

Wind
blowing
moving leaves
across the road
covering the ground.

Autumn colored leaves
red and orange
now faded
floating
down.

Soft
carpet
rustling loud
beneath my feet
I reach for my rake.

Trees reaching skyward
exposed branches
shivering
missing
clothes.

Change
occurs
intervals
marking seasons
soon winter will come.

Moon haiku

man in the moon stares

from a face made of green cheese

smiling down at me

Trees

Gathered together
green faces
marking ancient
vegetative races.

Branches
gnarled with age
heads bowed low
natural sage.

Knots like warts
scattered across
leafy branches
life's been rough.

Impervious to man
uncaring, aloof.

Trees do their own thing
they're morally proof.

Nodding in the breeze
arms eternally lifted
grasping at sun beams
enjoying what's been gifted.

Toes wiggled deep
deep-down in the dirt.
Cooling sweet comfort
tree roots never hurt.

Trunk pocket homes
in living, warm bark.
Sheltering small ones
in comforting dark.

Squirrels jumping
tree to tree to tree
carrying messages
delivering creeds.

Birds seek sanctuary
high off the ground.
Riding a leafy branch
as the rain pounds.

Building a nest
hatching their young.
Babes lulled into sleep
by chimes of wind song.

Shaded from the sun
sheltered from the rain
I am also part of the system
and will be again.

Filled with love

Little pink daisies,

A gift from me to you.

I wanted something special,

After all that we've been through.

These flowers are quite rare,

Don't you wonder why?

I grew them all by myself

No...I wouldn't lie.

Out there in my garden,

On that hallowed ground.

I've dedicated the whole patch,

By our friendship I am bound.

Each tiny, rosy petal,

Is filled with my love for you.

The scent is light and heavenly,

A single sniff will show my boast is true.

Will you accept my humble gift?

Given with my heart so true?

Or would you rather get,

Some flowers shaded blue?

Echo of Hard Rain haiku

echo of hard rain

slapping against the tin roof

makes me feel drowsy

Weed Whacking

Whacking weeds on Saturday
racing against the weather.
Mowing down an endless field
there is no greater pleasure.

Humming electric whacker
spraying rocks and sticks around.
A hundred foot power cord
that I drag across the ground.

A far off boom of thunder
dark clouds moving overhead.
I whack weeds from the corner
my hubby's already fled.

A bright, hot flash of lightning
stitching lines up in the sky.
I'm not done, I will not go
to quit now would make me cry.

In my haste some fire ants
In a nest I didn't see.
Are struck hard by the whacker
damn things land all over me.

A hundred little fires
make me scream and dance about.
The nasty little varmints
take my mind from my planned route.

The whacker falls from my hands
as the rain comes hurtling down.
Hubby opens up the door
his face wearing a big frown.

In his hands an umbrella
shielding him from the hard rain.
Calmly tugging the plug free
tells me I am such a pain.

Like a Drum haiku

splash of falling rain

beating my head like a drum

drowning out the wind

Mosquito?

Have you ever noticed
a mosquito
framed against the sky,
looks a little like a fairy,
with blood lust on its mind?
If you squint your eyes a little
you'll clearly see his horse
all four legs
as they dangle down
and a mane and tail of course.
Angry little fairy
manic beating wings
keeping horse aloft
as he swoops in for a swing.
Open little mouth
in a nearly silent little scream.
If you listen closely
you will hear his battle cry
voice so soft and low
like a newborn baby's sigh.
Look a little closer
see his tiny arm?
It's brandishing a sword.
Now I hear a buzzing sound
and back away alarmed.
I see the sword arm swing
before the first drop of blood is spilled
I have turned and run away.
My heart with fear is filled.
Perhaps I'll fight another day
if the fairy lives there still.

Country Drive

Driving along...
Singing a song...
heading out to the country.

Top rolled down....
freedom bound....
enjoying nature's bounty.

Took a break...
by a lake....
laid out in the sun.

Fell asleep...
in the heat...
sweat begin to run.

Face was red....
blisters tread....
across my lips and nose.

Couldn't breathe...
without a sneeze....
ragweed way too close.

Ants from lawn....
in my clothes drawn.....
The kind that like sting.

Jumped up fast
Removed pants
Ran through leafy brush.

Hornet nest....
hit my chest...
so embarrassing

Went in bra
My breasts raw
The pain breathtaking.

Ripped off shirt...
rolled in dirt....
screaming without pause.

Back to car...
wasn't far...
grateful it was close.

Put up top...
didn't stop...
Back to town I went.

Safely home....
all alone...
wounds still prominent!

Summertime is Fun Time

Summertime is fun time
So much to see and do
Barbecues to cook hamburgers
Swimming holes to ride on tubes.

Bare feet to walk the paths with
Cutoff jeans to keep our cool
the ice cream truck is fully stocked
frozen treats that make me drool.

Shade becomes a commodity
as we battle the constant heat.
Ice cold water melon eaten on the back porch
Spitting seeds down upon our feet.

Squirting each other with the water hose
Games of tag and volley ball
summertime feels so endless
there is no such thing as fall.

Scorching hot beach sand
Waves that you can ride
Theme parks and dinners out
Friend's together side by side

Night time's filled with lightning bugs
We'll go to the theater for a spooky treat
Popcorn, soda pop, and giggles
And all the goodies that you can eat.

Camping by the lake under the stars
listening to the creatures of the night
Huddled close around a small campfire
Feeling the delicious shivers of mutual fright

The days are going by so quickly
Soon July will be all over and done
Next month is August and although it's still summer
The dead hours of study and school will end the fun

Garden of Despair

Sitting on a wooden bench,
In my little garden of despair.
Watching all my worries growing fruit.
Although the sun is brightly shining,
All my hopes lay out there dying.
Seeing that my fears are taking root.
The clouds are darkly crying,
As my soul shrivels up inside.
Glancing at the newborn, tender shoots.
Why do I even bother trying?
I'm just a lonely little girl.
Peeking at the ugliness called truth.

The flavor of shame

Give me blue flowers,
A deep, intensive shade.
Make them scented,
The flavor of shame.
I turned my back on love,
It left me far behind.
I didn't know what I lost,
I was weak and blind.
Forgive me, and be my love...
Turn my life back to where it belongs
I've only got sad songs on the radio...
And blue flowers to remind me of what's gone.

Printed in Great Britain
by Amazon